P9-CSE-964

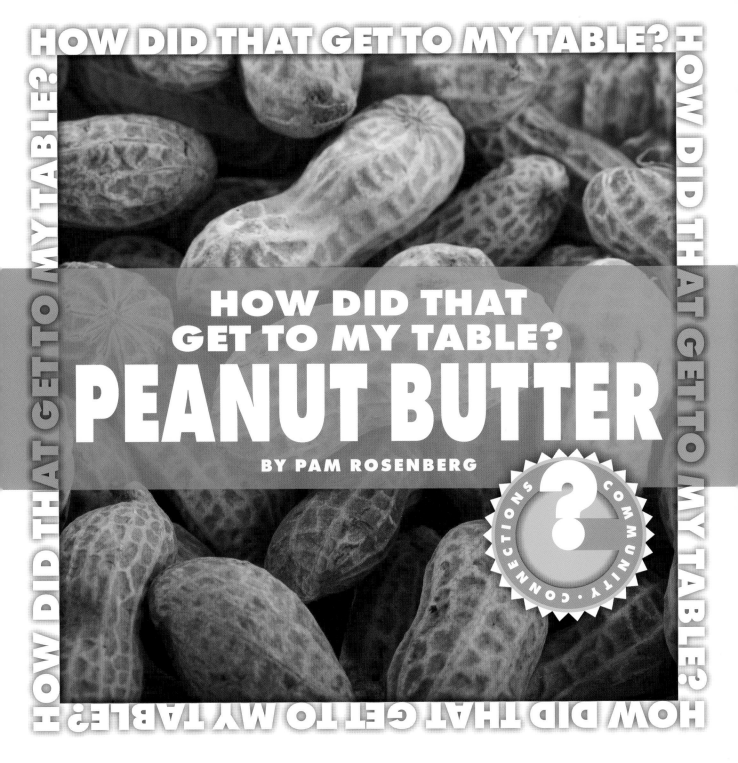

HOW DID THAT GET TO MY TABLE?
PEANUT BUTTER

BY PAM ROSENBERG

COMMUNITY CONNECTIONS

CHERRY LAKE
Publishing

Published in the United States of America by Cherry Lake Publishing
Ann Arbor, Michigan
www.cherrylakepublishing.com

Content Adviser: Barry G. Swanson, PhD, Professor and Interim Chair, School of Food Science, Washington State University
Reading Adviser: Cecilia Minden-Cupp, PhD, Literacy Consultant

Photo Credits: Cover, pages 1 and 11, ©wong yu liang, used under license from Shutterstock, Inc.; page 5, ©Hannamariah, used under license from Shutterstock, Inc.; page 7, ©Joe Gough, used under license from Shutterstock, Inc.; page 9, ©Wellford Tiller, used under license from Shutterstock, Inc.; page 13, ©Ian Patrick/Alamy; page 15, ©Stephen Aaron Rees, used under license from Shutterstock, Inc.; page 17, ©Steven May/Alamy; page 19, ©Grant Heilman Photography/Alamy; page 21, ©Blend Images/Alamy

LIBRARY OF CONGRESS CATALOGING-IN-PUBLICATION DATA
Rosenberg, Pam.
  How did that get to my table? Peanut butter / by Pam Rosenberg.
    p. cm.—(Community connections)
  Includes index.
  ISBN-13: 978-1-60279-469-6
  ISBN-10: 1-60279-469-3
  1. Peanut butter—Juvenile literature. I. Title. II. Title: Peanut butter. III. Series.
  TP438.P4R67 2009
  664'.726—dc22   2008052551

Cherry Lake Publishing would like to acknowledge the work of The Partnership for 21st Century Skills. Please visit *www.21stcenturyskills.org* for more information.

PEANUT BUTTER

CONTENTS

A NUTTY RIDDLE

It is tasty. Many people eat it with jelly. Sometimes it sticks to the roof of your mouth. What is it? Peanut butter!

Many people like to eat peanut butter. Did you ever wonder how peanut butter gets to your table?

Peanut butter tastes good with bread and with fruit.

FROM FARM TO FACTORY

The story of peanut butter begins at a peanut farm. Peanuts are planted in the spring. They grow underground. They are **harvested** in the fall.

These rows of peanut plants are growing in Australia.

Peanuts are just one kind of food that grows underground. Can you think of any other foods that grow underground? Hint: another food that grows underground is often eaten mashed or baked.

7

Picking machines dig the peanuts out of the ground. The peanuts are taken to a **warehouse**. A warehouse is a large building used to store things.

The peanuts are cleaned at the warehouse. Then they are stored in a **silo**. A silo is a tall, round tower.

A tractor pulls a machine called a combine. The combine helps harvest the peanuts.

Only peanut kernels are used to make peanut butter. The shells have to be removed. Big metal rollers crack the peanut shells. Other machines separate the peanut kernels from the shells.

The tasty peanut kernels are hidden inside tough, hard shells.

LOOK!

Look carefully at an unshelled peanut. What color is the peanut's shell? Is it bumpy or smooth? Looking at foods carefully is one way to learn more about them.

11

The shelled peanuts are often put into big sacks or boxes. Then they are loaded on trucks.

Truck drivers deliver the peanut kernels to peanut butter factories. That is where the peanuts will be made into peanut butter.

Bags of peanuts are stacked and ready to be loaded on trucks.

AT THE FACTORY

The peanuts are **roasted** at the factory. Roasted means they are baked in big ovens.

The peanuts are quickly cooled when they come out of the ovens. Then their skins are rubbed off.

Next, the peanuts are **inspected**. Any **scorched** or spoiled nuts are thrown away.

14

The skins of these peanuts will need to be rubbed off.

How are peanuts turned into peanut butter? Peanuts are fed into a **grinder**. The grinder crushes them into a smooth paste. Salt, sugar, and oil may be added during the grinding.

Then the peanut butter is put in a refrigerated container. It is called a **hopper**. The hopper mixes the peanut butter and cools it for **packaging**.

Look at the label on your peanut butter jar. It will tell you if salt, sugar, or oil were added to the peanuts.

Allergy advice

- **Recipe: Contains peanuts.**
  May contain traces of other nuts.

Ingredients

Whole Peanuts (91%), Sunflower Oil, Vegetable Fat, Salt.

Nutrition

Typical Composition. 100g contain:
Energy 2555kJ/620kcal, Protein 24.0g,
Carbohydrate 12.9g (of which sugars 3.2g),
Mono-unsaturates 24.8g, polyunsaturat
g), Fibre 6.9g, Sodium 0.3
Tablespoon typic

The last step at the factory is packaging the peanut butter. A machine packs the peanut butter into jars. Caps and labels are put on the jars. Then the jars are packed in boxes.

The boxes are loaded on trucks. The trucks carry the boxes to stores. That's where people like you can buy your favorite brand!

Machines can quickly fill many jars with peanut butter.

People who work in peanut butter factories must follow rules. These rules help make sure that peanut butter is safe to eat. What do you think some of the safety rules are? Hint: think about ways your family keeps food safe in your kitchen.

ON YOUR TABLE

You bring home a jar of peanut butter from the store. There is just one question left. How will you eat your peanut butter today?

Now you know how peanut butter got to your table!

GLOSSARY

grinder (GRINE-dur) a machine that crushes something into a smooth paste

harvested (HAR-vist-ed) to gather up crops that are ready for eating

hopper (HAH-pur) a rotating container that mixes peanut butter and cools it to the right temperature for packaging

inspected (in-SPEK-ted) looked at very carefully

packaging (PAK-ij-ing) putting a product in its container or wrapping

roasted (ROH-sted) baked in a hot oven

scorched (SKORCHD) burned

silo (SYE-loh) a tall, round tower used to store large amounts of foods such as nuts or grains

warehouse (WAIR-hous) a large building used for storing food or other products

FIND OUT MORE

BOOKS

Boten, Wallace. *From Farm to Store*. Minneapolis: Compass Point Books, 2004.

Keller, Kristin Thoennes. *From Peanuts to Peanut Butter*. Mankato, MN: Capstone Press, 2005.

WEB SITES

National Peanut Board—Fun Facts

www.nationalpeanutboard.org/classroom-funfacts.php
Read many fun facts about peanuts and peanut butter

Skippy—Kids Crafts

www.peanutbutter.com/bird_feeder.aspx
Learn how to make a bird feeder using pinecones and peanut butter

INDEX

ABOUT THE AUTHOR

Pam Rosenberg writes and edits nonfiction books for children. She lives with her family in Arlington Heights, Illinois. They usually have several jars of peanut butter in their pantry.

24